BUILDING

RESILIENCE

Rewire Your Brain, Think Your Way To A Better Life,

Develop A Strong Mental Foundation And Heal Your Life

To Create A New You.

Contents

Welcome!

I am so excited you have this book in your hands. I sincerely believe the more people take the benefits of resilience to heart, the better our world will be. When you take the time and have the determination to develop the primary success factors, I honestly feel pleased to be part of your success journey. Let's understand what this book is about.

During my childhood, I wondered why some people remain calm in the face of adversity while others crumble in pressure? Why do some people have high knowledge and required skills but fail to achieve their goals? Why do some people keep going, no matter what life throws at them? Later, I understood that the difference is simply the person's degree of resilience. The more resilient the person is, the more the power to face adversity. Even if you consider yourself a very competent person, you will inevitably encounter challenges at some point along your journey. Whenever you come across a challenging situation, you can either let your emotions get the best of you or become paralyzed by fear.

Building resilience is the key to turning challenges into successes. If you are resilient, these challenges may bend you, but they will not be able to break you. All of us have the power to develop a resilient mindset. Resilience mindset is like a muscle, which needs to be conditioned and strengthened every day. Sometimes it takes hitting your emotional threshold before you are able to tap into your personal resilience.

The first part of this book will give you in-depth knowledge and understanding of resilience, whereas the second part is about building resilience. People face many challenges or traumas in their lives. Sometimes they suffer a severe health issue or have been a victim of an assault or accident. Maybe they lost their job all of a sudden or lost a loved one. I am sure that this book will inspire and help you understand resilience and how to handle stress and trauma or any adverse situation in life. It provides a practical guide to building resilience and gives a direction to overcoming the adversities we all face at some point in our lives.

Introduction

When a baby tries to stand up, he falls several times before succeeding. When he tries to take a step forward, he falls and stumbles. The life cycle of a bird is similar to this. Its wings quiver as it makes its first attempts to fly. It tries and fails. But it does not give up. Finally, it spread its wings with one more try and succeeded. When an ant tries to climb a wall, it crawls a few inches and falls. But it keeps trying. In fact, the ant goes on trying infinitely, trying to reach the top of the wall. The ant keeps on trying till it reaches the top. In our entire life, we have succeeded numerous times after failures. We have learned riding cycles, driving cars, swimming, learning the alphabet, eating, managing business, managing relationships, winning losing games, etc.

In our lives, we come across situations where things don't go very well, which may be due to stress or other reasons. It is challenging for individuals to make some adjustments in their life, i.e., moving away from their comfort zone to something that might be difficult to adjust to in new scenarios. If we do not make changes in our practice, it will affect our day-to-day life and future. Therefore, when there are bad times, people who have acquired resilient skills have an increased chance of 'bouncing back.' This can reduce depression and other health issues.

When you have resilience, you harness inner strength that helps you rebound when you face a setback or challenge due to job loss, an illness, a disaster, a loved one's death, or others. If you lack resilience, you might dwell on problems, feel victimized, become overwhelmed, or turn to unhealthy coping mechanisms, such as substance abuse.

Resilience won't make your problems go away — but resilience helps to overcome the problem, find enjoyment in life, and better handle stress. If you are not as resilient as you would like to be, you can develop skills to become more resilient.

What Is Resilience?

Life is never a straight line, and everyone experiences ups and down, twists and turns, and even traumatic events in their life. These events affect people differently in terms of their thoughts, emotions, and life in general. But, people mainly adjust with time to these situations.

Resilience is the process of adapting well in the face of adversity, trauma, tragedy, failures, threats, health issues, family problems, or financial challenges.

Resilience refers to our ability to bounce back quickly to recover from adversity. If someone has not experienced adversity, there is no way to know if they are resilient at all. In other words, people who remain calm in the face of disaster have what psychologists call resilience. Resilient people are able to utilize their skills and strengths to cope and recover from problems and challenges.

Instead of falling into despair or hiding from problems, resilient people face life's difficulties head-on. This does not mean that they experience less distress, grief, or anxiety than other people do. It means that they use healthy coping skills to handle such challenges in ways that develop strength and growth. In many cases, they may emerge even stronger than they were before.

Disappointment or failure might drive them to unhealthy, destructive, or even dangerous behaviors. These individuals are slower to recover from setbacks and may experience more psychological distress as a result.

Resilience is what gives people the psychological strength to cope with stress and hardship. It is the mental reservoir of strength that people are able to call on in times of need to carry them through without falling apart. Psychologists believe that resilient individuals can better handle adversity and rebuild their lives after a struggle.

Dealing with change or loss is an inevitable part of life. At some point, everyone experiences varying degrees of setbacks. Some of these challenges might be relatively minor, while others are disastrous on a much larger scale.

How we deal with these problems can play a significant role in the outcome and the long-term psychological consequences. The good news is that resilience is a learnable skill. Acquiring greater resilience is like a muscle that can be exercised and made more robust day by day.

Resilience is categorized mainly as psychological resilience, emotional resilience, and physical resilience. Physical resilience refers to the physical ability to adapt to challenges, maintain stamina and strength, and recover quickly and efficiently. It plays an essential role in healthy aging, as people encounter medical issues and physical stressors. Daily walk out, engaging in physical sports activity, healthy lifestyle choices, building connections, deep breathing, and engaging in enjoyable activities all play a role in building physical resilience.

Psychological resilience refers to the ability to mentally withstand or adapt to uncertainty, challenges, and adversity. People who exhibit psychological resilience develop coping strategies and capabilities that enable them to remain calm and focused during a crisis and move on without long-term negative consequences.

People cope with stress and adversity differently. People are, by nature, more or less sensitive to change. How a person responds to a situation can trigger a flood of emotions. Emotionally resilient people understand what they're feeling and why. They tap into realistic optimism, even when dealing with a crisis, and are proactive in using both internal and external resources.

Besides, public resilience refers to the ability of groups of people to respond to and recover from adverse situations, such as natural disasters, pandemics, economic hardship, racial discrimination, and other challenges.

What Resilience Is Not

This is not true that a resilient person will not experience difficulty or distress. In fact, everyone will experience difficulties and distress, but a resilient person will be able to adapt to it and bounce back from the setback quickly.

Resilient is not the same for everyone. While everyone faces challenges or difficulties in life, how quickly they adapt to the situation depends on the degree of resilience of the person. Resilience involves behaviors, thoughts, and actions that anyone can learn and develop.

Resilience is a time-bound process; people can learn it. Like building a muscle, increasing your resilience takes time and requires regular intensity practice. Focusing on connection, wellness, healthy thinking, and meaning can empower you to withstand and learn from complex and traumatic experiences. You can use these strategies to increase your capacity for resilience to weather and grow from the difficulties.

Some people equate resilience with mental toughness, but demonstrating resilience includes working through emotional pain and suffering.

What Resilience Brings

Resilience involves "bouncing back" from these difficult experiences and brings profound personal development and growth. While these adverse events are undoubtedly painful and challenging, they don't have to determine the outcome of your life. You can control, modify, and grow with many aspects of your life. That's the role of resilience. Becoming more resilient helps you get through difficult circumstances and empowers you to grow and even improve your life along the way.

Resilient people experience stress, setbacks, and difficult emotions, but they tap into their strengths to overcome challenges and work through problems. Resilience empowers them to accept and adapt to a situation and move forward.

Why Is Resilience Important?

Resilience is what gives people the emotional strength to cope with trauma, adversity, and hardship. Resilient people utilize their resources, strengths, and skills to overcome challenges and work through setbacks.

People face all kinds of adversity in life. Personal crises include illness, loss of a loved one, abuse, bullying, job loss, and financial instability. People have to learn to cope with and work through challenging life experiences. Resilience is important because it gives people the strength to process and overcome hardship. Those lacking resilience get easily overwhelmed and may turn to unhealthy coping mechanisms. Resilient people tap into their strengths and support systems to overcome challenges and work through problems.

Resilience is essential for several reasons; it enables us to develop mechanisms for protection against experiences that could be overwhelming, helps us to maintain balance in our lives during difficult or stressful periods, and can also protect us from the development of some mental health difficulties and issues.

Resilience is the ability to adapt to challenging situations. When stress, adversity, or trauma strikes, you still experience anger, grief, and pain, but you are able to keep functioning — both physically and psychologically. Resilience is what helps you to persevere through difficulties, stay focused amid distractions, and to coast more easily when your life is calmer. Some people are more naturally resilient than others. Most of us, however, have to work at it.

Resilience isn't a fixed trait. Flexibility, adaptability, and perseverance can help people tap into their resilience by changing specific thoughts and behaviors. Developing resilience is both complex and personal. It involves a combination of inner strengths and external resources, and there isn't a universal formula for becoming more resilient. All people are different: While one person might develop symptoms of depression or anxiety following a traumatic event, another person might not report any symptoms at all.

A combination of factors contributes to building resilience, and there isn't a simple to-do list to work through adversity. In one longitudinal study, protective factors for adolescents at risk for depression, such as family cohesion, positive self-appraisals, and good interpersonal relations, were associated with resilient outcomes in young adulthood.

Resilience is our ability to adapt and bounce back when things do not go as planned. Resilient people do not dwell on failures; they acknowledge the situation, learn from their mistakes, and move forward.

Essential Elements To Resilience

The fact is that everyone fails from time to time. Making mistakes is an inevitable part of living. The only way to avoid this is never trying anything new or taking a risk. Even that also does not guarantee not facing any challenges.

Resilient people view a difficulty as a challenge. They look at their failures and mistakes as lessons to be learned from and growth opportunities. They do not view them as a negative reflection on their abilities or self-worth.

Resilient people are committed to their lives and their goals. Besides their goals, they commit to their relationships, their friendships, the causes they care about, and their religious or spiritual beliefs.

Resilient people spend their time and energy focusing on situations and events that they have control over. They do not spend time worrying about uncontrollable events can often feel lost, helpless, and powerless to take action. Instead, they put their efforts to feel confident and having the most impact.

What Does Resilience Provide?

Resilience does not eliminate stress or erase life's difficulties. People who possess this quality don't see life through rose-colored lenses; they understand that setbacks happen and that sometimes, life is hard and painful. They still experience the negative emotions that come after a tragedy, but their mental outlook allows them to work through these feelings and recover.

Resilience gives people the strength to tackle problems head-on, overcome adversity, and move on with their lives. In the wake of various natural disasters, many individuals demonstrated behaviors that resemble resilience—and they experienced fewer symptoms of depression as a result. Resilience is the result of a complex series of internal and external characteristics, including genetics, physical fitness, mental health, and environment.

What Are The Impacts?

People who lack resilience are more likely to feel distressed and hopeless and practice unhealthy coping strategies. One study showed that patients who had attempted suicide had significantly lower resilience scale scores than patients who had never attempted suicide.

Students experience a tremendous amount of physical and mental growth on a daily basis. Between school, co-curricular activities, work, and social life, teens face many new experiences and challenges. Being resilient gives them the ability to tackle this head-on, bounce back from any setbacks and have the best chance at succeeding. It allows them to learn and grow in all situations. Resilience also helps them face new situations, people, or experiences with confidence and a positive mindset, making them more likely to be successful in life. Resilient people see bad events' effects as temporary rather than permanent.

Mental Toughness And Resilience

People often consider mental toughness and resilience the same, but they are actually not technically identical. Mental toughness and resilience are often colloquially used to refer to each other. In fact, resilience is commonly considered a process.

Resilience gives us all kinds of mental and psychological strengths. Adversity in health, family, work or any area of your life could be right around the corner. Resilience consists of the mental processes and behaviors that people use to protect themselves from the harmful effects of stressors. It's the ability to adapt and flex to the obstacles that life continuously presents.

Adversity and stress are a part of life, but our responsibility is to respond. We can succumb to the stress or rise to the occasion to explore ways to bounce back. We can treat resilience like planning for an oncoming storm that helps diffuse the storm's power. Some people are naturally resilient. Others may need to build resilience skills to better weather the storm.

We typically think of resilience as the ability to "bounce back" or recover from disappointment. It's much deeper than this. To go through a trial of some kind and simply "bounce back" to your original position shows a lack of evolution and growth. When people are not resilient, they usually give up when they face adversity because they didn't experience pain in their life. Resilience is nothing more than a decision; it's a mindset on how you see growth.

Failure Makes You Resilient

When we are confronted with failure, we see all the negative aspects that come with it. We entirely discount the benefits of failing. Each failure provides the opportunity to grow stronger. Failure offers the chance to return stronger, wiser, and smarter than we were before. More than that, failure makes the person more resilient and strengthens the belief system.

Elon Musk once said, "When you first start a company, there's lots of optimism, and things are great. Happiness, at first, is high. Then, you encounter all sorts of issues, and happiness will steadily decline, and you'll go through a whole world of hurt." But, if you take your medicine and learn from your failures, there's an upside. "Eventually, if you succeed … you will finally get back to happiness," says Musk. He believes failure is necessary on the path of success, and overcoming failure brings a new you in the form of resilience.

Nelson Mandela said, "Do not judge me by my successes; judge me by how many times I fell down and got back up again."

We allow failure to discourage us. But the great people like Thomas A. Edison take it differently. Edison said, "I have not failed. I've just found 10,000 ways that won't work."

Abraham Lincoln failed in business, suffered a nervous breakdown, and was defeated in eight elections. The more he faced failures, the more resilient he became as he refused to stop trying his best. Lincoln was elected in 1861 as the 16th President of the United States of America. He said, "My great concern is not whether you have failed, but whether you are content with your failure." The amount of rejection you receive is not a defining factor. Success is still within your reach.

Steven Spielberg, one of the most influential filmmakers of all time, is a familiar household name. Spielberg has directed more than fifty films and has been awarded three Oscars. But, he was rejected from the University of Southern California three times due to low grades in high school. Spielberg had made many mistakes that he knew were unacceptable, yet in the end, his film succeeded. Perseverance and acceptance of failure is the key to success, after all. He said, "Even though I get older, what I do never gets old, and that's what I think keeps me hungry."

Colonel Sanders is the founder of Kentucky Fried Chicken (KFC). It wasn't until the age of 62 that Sanders, with a $105 social security check in hand, pitched his chicken recipe to restaurants. It is estimated that he had knocked on more than a thousand doors before getting his first order. How many of us quit after three tries, ten tries, a hundred tries, and then we say we tried as hard as we could? Instead of giving up, he hit the road and began trying to sell his franchise-model chicken restaurant, eventually finding success with a restaurant outside Utah. It became the first Kentucky Fried Chicken, and the restaurant tripled sales in a year, mainly from the colonel's chicken.

Walt Disney, Mickey Mouse's creator, dropped out of school at a young age in a failed attempt at joining the army. His Laugh-o-Gram Studios went bankrupt due to his lack of ability to run a successful business. He was once fired from a Missouri newspaper for "not being creative enough." During his initial days, he faced many rejections from newspaper editors, who said he had no talent. Disney was working out of a tiny mouse-infested shed near the church. After seeing a small mouse, he was inspired. That was the start of Mickey Mouse.

The famous bestselling American author, Stephen King, was a paranoid, troubled child tormented by nightmares and raised in poverty. But he grew up to the title "Master of Horror." He worked from a makeshift desk in the laundry room of his double-wide trailer. He was too poor to buy his own; he had to borrow a typewriter from his wife, who worked the second shift at Dunkin' Donuts to help pay the bills for their struggling family of four. Stephen was a struggling author and faced depression because of his early failures, but he had tremendous belief in his skills even when everyone around him left his side. Stephen King's life is a lesson that teaches us how repeated challenges in life made him resilient and bolstered his belief system to become one of the most successful persons in history.

These examples show that failure is compelling, enhancing realism, creativity, and resilience.

How To Drive Resilience

The fact is that we're going to fail from time to time: it's an inevitable part of living that we make mistakes and occasionally fall flat on our faces. The only way to avoid this is to live a shuttered and meager existence, never trying anything new or taking a risk. Few of us want a life like that!

Building better resilience takes time, effort, commitment, and focus. It's a process that will take months to learn and master. Don't give up and lose your patience. Resilience is a skill that you can readily enhance with patience and training.

This setback is an opportunity to be resilient. Instead of feeling broken, stand right up and face reality. Feel calm and relaxed from within as well, instead of a fake reassuring smile on the outside.

Despite struggling with "failure" throughout his entire working life, Edison never let it get the best of him. His resilience gave the world some of the most amazing inventions of the early 20th century, such as the phonograph, the telegraph, and the motion picture.

It's hard to imagine what our world would be like if Edison had given up after his first few failures. His inspiring story forces us to look at our own lives – do we have the resilience that we need to overcome our challenges? Do we let our failures upset our dreams? What could we accomplish if we had the strength not to give up?

When you have resilience, you harness inner strength that helps you rebound from a setback or challenge, such as a job loss, an illness, a disaster, or a loved one's death. If you lack resilience, you might dwell on problems, become overwhelmed, and feel victimized.

Resilience won't make your problems go away — but resilience can give you the ability to see past them, find enjoyment in life, and better handle stress. If you aren't as resilient as you'd like to be, you can develop skills to become more resilient.

Resilience is developed by standing up and facing every challenge, big and small, without striking out or running away from it. We stand and endure the most significant assaults, the greatest pain, the deadliest disease, the most powerful enemy, and anything else that our life can throw at us. In the subsequent chapters, all common methods of developing resilience are explained.

Remember Your Why

I used to quote this example to explain the importance of the purpose. Once the mountain people in the Andes invaded the lowlanders, and as part of their plundering of the people, they kidnapped a baby of one of the lowlander families and took the infant with them back up into the mountains.

The lowlanders didn't know how to climb the mountain. They didn't know where to find the mountain people or track them in the steep terrain. Even then, they sent out their best fighting men to climb the mountain and bring the baby home.

First, the men tried one method of climbing and then another. They tried one track and then another. However, after several days of effort, they had climbed only a couple of hundred feet. Hopeless, the lowlander men decided that the cause was lost, and they prepared to return to their village below. As they were packing their gear for the descent, they saw the baby's mother walking toward them. They realized that she was coming down the mountain, which they hadn't figured out how to climb.

And then they saw that she had the baby strapped to her back. How could that be? One man greeted her and said, "We couldn't climb this mountain. How did you do this when we, the strongest and ablest men in the village, couldn't do it?" She shrugged her shoulders and said, "It wasn't your baby."[1]

Imagine your doctor warning you that you will die in 6 months of a heart attack if you don't do a one-hour daily workout. What will you do? Without a doubt, you will go to the gym every day because your purpose is clear – to save your life. You won't get into a building set on fire. But if your kid is stuck in that fire, you don't need any motivation or discipline to rush towards that. Therefore, the first thing is to define your purpose.

____

[1] *https://purposefocuscommitment.com/inspirational-story-have-purpose-motivation-perseverance/*

If your purpose motivates you, you will not depend much on motivation. Otherwise, you will just find ways to drag yourself to the task. The purpose is a magnet that pulls you towards itself.

Why Is Purpose So Important?

If a person does not have a vital purpose or reason for the goal, it is tough to restart when the momentum drops. The person needs to ask why he wants to achieve his goals. The reasons are the fuel that will keep him burning. The reasons must be intense and emotional enough to get them moving. If the purpose for their goal is not strong enough, they will not do whatever it takes to achieve the goal. Their reasoning can reignite your desire and keep your motivation high.

Action-taking is the key to success. To become motivated to take massive action, you need to have a purpose and get emotional about it. To let the motivation take root and lodge itself in your brain, you have to practice and remind yourself of your purposes. You have to remind yourself of your purpose and get emotional about it as often as possible. This is how successful high-performers take massive action: They repeat their goals to themselves multiple times a day and think about them. You need to do visualizations, affirmations, pictures of your goals, or triggers that set off your emotions all-around your workspace. And then you have to interact with them multiple times a day. If you follow that process, you will want to take massive action and not need any other motivation. It takes time but is worth it.

How Does Purpose In Life Make People Resilient?

Recognizing your purpose helps you focus your energy, keeps you engaged, makes it easier to be hopeful, fills you with courage, and improves resilience. Purpose can come from the pursuit to help other people or abide by a set of values. Hence, when things get tough in life, revisit the reasons why you think what you are attempting is essential. That will reconnect you to your original motivation. Having a purpose makes it easier to bounce back in challenging times by providing perspective, stability, confidence, and determination. It is much harder to be defeated when you are passionate and purposeful about your journey.

The purpose is essential to resilience. People who have a clear purpose and direction for their lives find it much easier to keep moving forward. People with purpose are known to be more resilient. While some people get knocked down and stay right there, resilient people bounce back from their misery with a smile on their face and move forward. Research studies also indicate that if we live with purpose, we live longer, have better health, and make better lifestyle choices.

One of the common traits among people who live with purpose is that they are able to find meaning and learn in all of life's experiences which make them emotionally resilient. This happens particularly when confronting life's challenges offers a psychological buffer against obstacles. Having a purpose allows you to bounce forward by improving your life for the better and enabling you to continue to deal with challenges successfully moving forward.

Purpose in life also leads to both improved health and longevity. People who think their life has meaning are more likely to make a conscious effort to look after their health and wellbeing. Being purpose-driven won't add more hours to your day, but it will give you the strength and energy to not be so worn down by workplace demands.

The purpose is clearly an asset for promoting resilience in the face of adversity. Purpose in life predicts both health and longevity suggesting that the ability to find meaning from life's experiences, especially when confronting life's challenges, may be a mechanism underlying resilience. Having a purpose in life may motivate reframing stressful situations to deal with them more productively, thereby facilitating recovery from stress and trauma. Overall, people with a greater sense of purpose generally experience greater mental wellbeing and are far less likely to suffer more common mental health issues such as depression and anxiety.

Believe In Yourself

"Whether you think you can, or you think you can't — you're right"– Henry Ford

Such thoughts are the basis of our beliefs. Henry Ford recognized the critical role of our beliefs in our success and happiness. The greatest obstacle toward achieving success in your life is the inability to believe that success is possible. Many do not have a complete sense of their belief, what they can or can't achieve. They cannot see the greatness within, nor do they believe they can achieve whatever they put their minds to. This is a major reason they do not set goals, for they do not believe they will ever achieve them. Their attitude affects their self-esteem.

Belief in your own ability to cope with life's challenges plays an integral part in resilience. Becoming more confident and your ability to respond to and deal with a crisis is a great way to build resilience for the future.

Believing in yourself means having confidence in your own abilities. It means trusting yourself to do what you say you'll do and knowing that those efforts will result in the desired outcomes. When we believe in ourselves, it kicks into gear all sorts of psychological processes that help us achieve our goals, manifest our dreams, and increase our well-being. But the flip side is also true. Lack of self-confidence or belief in ourselves means we are less likely to act, change, or push to improve things. As a result, we are actually more likely to fail when we expect to fail. That means that believing in ourselves is kind of like the key that turns the ignition and starts the car. We can't really go anywhere without it.

We must be careful while focusing on self-belief to build resilience. We must be realistic about our capabilities, as near to the real self. If we overestimate our abilities, it may lead to over-confidence, arrogance and may lead us to take higher, calculated risks.

Belief And Resilience

Does our belief in ourselves help us come out of challenges, or do they make us more vulnerable and cause us to succumb to the challenges? When you build strong self-belief and confidence, you start defining your values and beliefs and living those in everything you do. That deep self-belief becomes resilience. That resilience will not stop fear, disappointment, or hurt when things don't work out. That is part of the beautiful, emotional spectrum of human nature. What confidence and resilience do together is to keep you feeling hopeful.

While our fears and doubts about situations or circumstances are essential for survival, we grow as individuals every time we face our fears or do something we are afraid to do. We prove to ourselves that we have the capability to face adversity and come out resilient. The more adversities we face, the more skills we acquire, which builds our confidence and resources to come out of similar situations effectively. This confidence gives us a sense of control over the situation.

Sometimes nobody remains there to help you out from challenging situations. So it is essential to master all the strength you have and take the first step towards the problem to face it. When your negative thoughts come into your mind, practice immediately replacing them with positive ones, such as, "I can do this," "I'm good at my job," I will be successful," etc.

When a person has self-belief, automatically degree of resilience increases very much. Learning from mistakes was a significant predictor of coping and confidence, tenacity and adaptation, and tolerance to adverse situations. Self-belief is our belief in our capabilities to direct our efforts for the desired outcome. Our confidence in our ability to deal positively with everything that life throws at us is our confidence.

Once we challenge our self-belief, we look at the situation differently and respond to it differently. We use our belief as a reframing strategy.

Beliefs Have An Enormous Impact!

Resilient people have a strong belief system. They hold positive beliefs about themselves, letting them thrive. They believe in themselves and their ability. They don't wait for their luck but in their ability to craft their own destiny.

Everyone has thousands of beliefs about themselves, other people, politics, religion, the world, etc. We take most of our beliefs for granted and rarely consider whether or not they are helpful.

When we view various events and the world around us, we do so through the lenses of our beliefs. In other words, our view is not reality but an interpretation of our beliefs. This can be very limiting when we have a negative thinking style and view everything through negative lenses. We fail to see or hear positives because our negative lens filters them out.

When you believe in luck only, you will be reluctant to put in any effort. If you believe that you can't achieve, there seems little point in even trying.

Belief Creates Resilience

Belief doesn't just survive adversity; it gets stronger because of it. Belief empowers people by giving them unshakable resolve. Belief is the ability to respond to any situation with extraordinary toughness, tenacity, and determination.

Because of the belief system, top performers maintain a laser focus on what needs to be done in response to adversity. They do not waste time, or energy complaining, worrying, or excusing. They focus all their attention and energy on doing what needs to be done. They never quit, give in, and give up mindset. When it gets more challenging, they get better.

When difficult situations hit, belief does something compelling. It sustains your vision and strengthens your will. It makes you stronger because of the adversity you are forced to endure.

Belief Ignites And Activates

Your belief determines how much access you have to your capabilities when you are under pressure. Most people work very hard to develop capabilities but sometimes fail to take full advantage of those capabilities because doubt, distractions, and negative thinking hold them back.

Belief has laser focus, and it eliminates doubt and distractions. Therefore, belief is the ignition that actuates your ability to operate at max capability. Belief is the trigger that empowers you to perform at the highest level. Positive, powerful beliefs are vital if you want to thrive. They make you stronger, more confident, and more resilient.

Belief ignites and activates everything. Talent and training are not enough. The highest levels of performance require the deepest levels of belief. It is said that the elite win in their mind first.

What Is A Belief System?

Many factors contribute to success, but one of the essential factors is the belief system. A person's achievement mostly depends on how strong his belief system is. Many times, the difference in whether you succeed or not comes down to one simple thing, i.e., belief system. Every human being has strengths and weaknesses, but our mind is most inclined to the weaknesses or negativities such as anxiety, problems, or difficulties instead of choosing to believe in our natural ability to overcome the challenges.

A belief system is how much a person believes in himself. This is very important because it builds a person's self. It comprises values, skills, knowledge, and abilities. A person without a strong belief system constantly downplays their abilities, and in most cases, they achieve less because they do not believe that they could have done better. On the other hand, a person with a strong belief system knows their worth and value.

For instance, when people with no self-belief or are low in self-belief see a job opportunity with their skills, they may half-heartedly behave because they believe that they are not good enough for the job. On the other hand, people with self-belief will pursue the job wholeheartedly because they believe they are well-qualified.

Everyone desires success, but it does not come to everybody. The most crucial difference between successful and unsuccessful people is whether they believe in themselves. Successful people are more determined about their goals, and they try to make the best out of every favorable opportunity which comes to them in any situation.

In the end, people without self-belief or self-confidence may end up working a much lower job category than what they deserve. Meanwhile, people with self-belief will move from that job to a better one and might eventually reach a much higher level.

This small example indicates that while self-belief might seem inconsequential or very insignificant, but it can adversely affect our entire lives both directly and indirectly.

Embrace Change To Develop Resilience

"If you want life to change, you have to change. If you want life to be better, you have to be better"—Jim Rohn

Life changes constantly, and sometimes it is difficult to realize that changes are happening continuously at every moment. Change is an inevitable part of life. Even if we do not perceive changes every time, continuous changes are happening in us, others, and the environment. Every moment, along with the date and time, our age is increasing, the physiology and psychology of every person change every moment. The behavior, the attitude, the response, the thought process, the environment, everything within and outside of us change with time and circumstances. In fact, life is constantly changing. Life never stays the same. Our circumstances change; our work, social life, health, family dynamics, and everything changes. Good times come, and good times go. Bad times come, and bad times go. Most people try to resist those changes, but mentally strong people focus on coping with a fast-changing reality. They say that the only thing constant in life is change. As a result of difficult circumstances, specific goals may no longer be realistic or attainable. Accepting goals that you cannot change allows you to focus on the things you do have control over.

So how do we go about achieving resilience? How would they go about it if someone wanted to make a change or progress in life? Everything in life comes as a choice. In many cases, you are just making a choice. Like when you decide to spend your time studying instead of chit-chatting with friends, you choose that. Similarly, you decide to excel in a job by spending more time on creative thinking and innovation in work instead of doing a normal routine job and going home.

Whenever any changes are perceived, what do you think? What would your reaction be? What questions come to your mind? What would you respond? What would your self-talk at that time? Would you be energized or stressed? Most people experience some level of change every day, whether positive or negative.

Life, as the saying goes, is full of surprises. Unemployment, employment, new relationships, breakups, new opportunities, missed opportunities, death, and new life. It is a never-ending series of meandering twists and turns that can bring happiness at best, heart-wrenching sadness at worst, and everything in between. Just like life's surprises are inevitable, so are its never-ending waves of change and transformation.

Many aspects of the changing world are outside your individual control. Different people perceive changes in different ways. For some people, change is an energizer, a motivator; and they seek out change and appear to thrive on change. For other people, change is experienced as exhausting and demotivating. Knowing how change affects you can help determine your own strategies that will allow you to be resilient in the face of the often constant changes we face in our personal and professional lives.

Impact Of Change

Whether changes are small or large, it impacts the work you do. You need to be resilient to manage your own response to the change. When you are stressed, your emotions can take over, and you are not able to think at your highest level. In the book "The Power of Now," Eckhart Tolle said, "The present moment is sometimes unacceptable, unpleasant or awful. As explained in The Power of Now, much of our negativity arises from a denial of the present moment. Unease, anxiety, tension, stress, worry (all forms of fear) are caused by too much focus on the future and not enough on the present. Guilt, regret, resentment, grievances, sadness, bitterness, and all forms of non-forgiveness are caused by too much focus on the past and not enough on the present. Therefore, the starting point is to accept where you are now and focus on what choices are open to you in relation to dealing with what you are faced with at this point in time—accepting that you are facing a challenge in the present moment and taking responsibility for your own circumstances.

How Change Is Related To Resilience

The best way to handle change is to accept that change is a part of life. Certain goals, ideals, or targets cannot be attainable due to adverse situations or circumstances in life. Accepting circumstances or situations that cannot be changed can help you focus on circumstances that you can control or alter.

Resilience is the ability to adapt well in the face of challenges. It allows oneself to bounce back after hardship. When you face a life crisis, you will be better equipped to respond if you know how to be more adaptable. While the changes may crumble some people, resilient people are able to adapt and thrive.

You are resilient when you understand your own and others' reactions to the change and when you are able to recognize when your stress levels are getting higher, and you need to do something to reduce it.

Individuals with growth mindsets stretch themselves, accept feedback and take the long view. An openness to hard work, risk, and even the prospect of failure provide foundational aspects for cultivating change resilience. To develop a growth mindset, become aware of the personal narrative in your head.

How To Embrace Change

The changes are so frequent; we need to find ways to be resilient in the face of this kind of significant change. The most crucial factor contributing to personal resilience through change is awareness about the change.

Awareness is essential because change is often accompanied by high levels of stress that can affect our lives at home and work front. We are resilient when we understand the impact of change and when we can recognize the stress levels are getting too high and do something to reduce it.

We need to develop our mindset in such a way that we can plan for at least some of the predictable changes in our life. Like buying insurance, you need to create a mindset open to change — you hope you won't need to use it, but you want to safeguard yourself for the future.

Many things in your life which you can't control. When you start accepting this and keep doing hard work, you will gain tons of experience. This is the first step in building resilience.

While it is helpful during times of difficulty to remember the old adage that "this too shall pass," this also means that good times will pass, so change is the only constant in life. Accepting change as inevitable in life helps us achieve happiness because it strengthens our ability to be content with the present moment and gives us the strength to grow in the future.

Since our birth and throughout our entire life, we have faced a number of challenges. How we perceive and process challenges are actually more important than the actual situation. In fact, adverse events only negatively impact when we negatively respond to them. A positive response neutralizes the negative effect. Having an internal locus of control and reframing negative events to find a positive purpose is actually more critical than whether or not we experience these stressful events in life. We can influence the outcome of our life when we believe that we can control our life rather than when we believe that we have no control over it. Control improves motivation, decreases anxiety, performs better under stress, experience less stress during times of difficulty, and improves overall psychological well-being.

The important point is that when you complain about a situation, it implies non-acceptance, and by complaining, you accept that you are a victim of the situation. When you change the situation by taking action, you are taking back your personal power and responsibility. When taking action, any action is often better than no action, especially if you have been held in an unhappy situation for a long time. By doing something, you will learn something, and this will lead you to a different place with different choices; doing nothing reveals nothing. If fear is stopping you from taking action, feel the fear and do it anyway.

Focus On Skill Development

Skills are essential in the progress of life. To become successful in life, you need to gain mastery of some skills. It may be leadership skills, problem-solving skills, communication skills, public speaking skills, or any subject-specific skills. The more skills you have, the more will be the resilience to achieve the goals in life. Take the example of any successful persons in any field, they are highly skilled in that particular field, and they acquire those skills by relentless learning and practicing.

Resilience may take time to build; many times, people get discouraged if they struggle to cope with problematic events. Everyone can learn to be resilient, and it doesn't involve any specific set of behaviors or actions. Resilience can vary dramatically from one person to the next. One way of developing resilience is developing skills. Developing resilience skills can help you face challenges and difficulties in life, which can help you feel better and cope better. Focus on practicing these skills and the common characteristics of resilient people, but also remember to build on your existing strengths.

Research suggests that people who are able to come up with solutions to a problem are better able to cope with problems than those who cannot. Whenever you encounter a new challenge, make a quick list of potential ways to solve the problem.

Experiment with different strategies and develop a logical way to work through common problems. By practicing your problem-solving skills regularly, you will be better prepared to cope when a serious challenge emerges. Your level of resilience determines how quickly you get back up. It helps you push through life's circumstances and meet challenges head-on.

I give a simple example of how resilience develops. When you first try to play volleyball, your hands get sore and swelled up. Some may even quit after the second or third occasion. But if you continue, your hands become stronger, and soon you find the process becomes effortless and enjoyable. In essence, your hands become more resilient with more practice. The more you play, the more will be the strength of your hands. This tells that resilience is a character, and strength can be developed.

A resilient person pushes past that initial discomfort and soon begins to realize that there are greater joy and satisfaction ahead. When a person is skillful, the confidence level remains high. And when confidence is high, the person will not give up easily; resilience is visible to fight more.

Scale Your Skills

Today, the only way to rise to the top is to improve yourself and add to your skills constantly. Even when you are at the top, you need to improve your skill to remain there. Take the example of Magnus Carlsen, who reigns the chess world for a decade and looks invincible. That requires continuous learning at the top level and evolving accordingly.

Skills are attached with the value in the current job market. The more skills you have, the more valuable you become to both employers and society. Scaling your skills or sharpening your skills boosts your confidence and significantly improves your perseverance and resilience. Continual learning and practicing those learnings will take you to that height. Life has full of challenges at whatever level or stages you are in. It throws challenges, and your role is to develop or upgrade your skills to face the challenges, which supports you to become resilient and ultimately succeed.

A well-developed skill can make us master a particular field, and it can be learned too. Learning new skills helps in your professional life a lot. It helps you achieve your goals, gives confidence, and motivates you to work too.

What Is Skills Development?

Skills development is identifying the skill gaps and improving these skills. It is important because your skills determine your ability to execute your plans with success.

Imagine a soldier carrying the most modernized weapons to fight a war. But he does not have the skills to use the weapons. Without that skills, the weapons are useless; he can't fight for a win. But if a soldier is skilled to fight, even if he has a less modernized weapon, he will be in a better position to win the war.

It's the same with goal achievement. In goal achievement, your skills are your tools. Just as you need the right tools to build a house, you need the right skills to achieve your goal. Without the right skills, you will spend a lot of time dealing with rudimentary issues caused by the lack of knowledge or skills and end up with unsatisfactory results. Although challenges are part and parcel of any goal achievement, you find yourself struggling harder without the right skills.

People are often impressed by what others have accomplished without realizing what they went through to reach there. They only see their accolades and victories, and most of them fail to realize their efforts and hard work. In short, when we see others' successes, what we don't see are the countless hours they spent behind the scenes honing their skills. Skills development is where we turn from beginner to intermediate to expert.

Likewise, if you are starting a new goal, it's about building your skills first. The best coach wasn't born with coaching skills; he learns them. The best musician wasn't born with the skill to play musical instruments; he learns it. All these are skills that are developed consciously. Every person can do the same.

Build Your Resilience By Facing Fear

Most of us get scared when we come across difficulties. It is normal, but how we handle the fear and come out of it makes you stronger. Just remember your first journey alone in an unknown distant place or the first time you are delivering a public speech or presentation at school; you might have had butterflies in your stomach. But once you cross the fear, it becomes easier, and you discover yourself.

Fear plays a significant role in preventing us from being resilient. We are afraid that is why we often run away from facing difficult situations. But facing our fears is a key in building resilience because we have to stop avoiding negative emotions. Being afraid is normal, but standing up to what scares us is essential if we want to overcome challenges healthily and adaptively.

When we are able to tackle the things that scare us and eventually even overcome them, it gives us a feeling of confidence and self-reliance. Fear no longer rules the day. It's self-knowledge that says, "I can do this." The more we do this, the more skilled we get at facing our fears. Not because the world becomes a less scary place, but because we have the confidence that we can do what we need to do to overcome the fear that may be otherwise holding us back. Learning to face our fears is a powerful and essential element of resilience.

The more practice we get at overcoming our fears, the better prepared we are for facing whatever happens in our life. As our resilience grows stronger, we are better prepared for future adversity.

Fear And Resilience

Fear is an image of something that has not happened yet, and most likely never will. So if you are serious about manifesting and want to manifest your goals faster, you should definitely face your fear. Or at least accept them and still take action. When I first entered the professional world, I was always hesitant to take ownership and do the routine work that most others were doing. Initially, I feared what others would say. Later, I understood that you empower yourself and improve your productivity by taking ownership of any activities. With this, your authority increases automatically, and a message goes to the other team members, be it your seniors, colleagues, or juniors. Slowly, you start realizing that you are the captain of the ship. All others are just the passengers—your value in the organization increases, which impacts your career and the organization. A person will never take enough care of a rented car or rented house. Only when he owns a house or a car or anything, he starts taking extra care. Mark Twain rightly said, "Almost any man worthy of his salt would fight to defend his home, but no one ever heard of a man going to war for his boarding house."

Resilience is nothing but understanding your fears and response in a crisis which ultimately helps you be more prepared and better able to heal whatever damage is done. We are all similar in that; we're much more resilient than we realize. We learn and grow but do not always give ourselves credit for coming through the tough times.

Understanding your fears and how you respond to a crisis can help you be more prepared and better able to heal whatever damage is done. That's resilience. We're all similar in that we're much more resilient than we realize. We learn and grow but don't always give ourselves credit for coming through the tough times.

The only way to become fearless in pursuing your dreams and goals is to face the fear straight. Every challenging situation that creates fear in you brings you an opportunity to overcome it and boost your confidence. If you avoid facing the fear, it becomes more extensive with time. Half of the fear vanishes if you face them and accept them. This sounds simple but requires much courage to remind yourself that you have accepted it every time. Often when we set big goals for ourselves, it is easy to get overwhelmed and be fearful of failure. In these instances, it is essential to gather your courage and keep going, one step at a time. Most people avoid their fears. But mentally strong people have nothing to prove, so they confront and overcome the fears to create an updated version of themselves.

In short, learning to face our fears is a powerful and essential element of resilience. The more practice we get at overcoming our fears, the better prepared we are for facing whatever happens in our life. As our resilience grows stronger, we are better prepared for future adversity.

In fact, fear helps you instinctively protect yourself from harm. Your fear might help you recognize when you're about to do something dangerous, and it could help you make a safer choice. But, you might find yourself fearful of things that aren't actually dangerous, like public speaking.

Fear, Confidence, And Resilience

When you are able to challenge the things that scare you and eventually even overcome them, it improves your self-confidence and resilience. When you face your fears and try difficult things, you will gain confidence in yourself. The more you do this, the more skilled you get at facing your fears. This is not because the world becomes a less scary place, but because you have developed the confidence to overcome the fear that may be otherwise holding you back. Learning to face fears is a powerful and essential element of resilience.

The more practice you do to overcome your fears, the better prepared you are for facing whatever happens in your life. As your resilience grows stronger, you are better prepared for future adversity.

The Consequence Of Avoiding Fears

"Every time your fear is invited up, every time you recognize it and smile at it, your fear will lose some of its strength." - Thich Nhat Hanh

The only way to deal with fear is to face it. Avoiding fears only prevent you from moving forward and makes you anxious. The best way to build your confidence is by facing your fears head-on.

Practice facing some of your fears that stem from a lack of self-confidence. Even if you are afraid you will embarrass yourself or think that you will mess up, try it anyway. Tell yourself it's just an experiment and see what happens.

You might learn that being a little anxious or making a few mistakes isn't as bad as you thought. And each time you move forward, you can gain more confidence in yourself, which in the end, will help prevent you from taking any risks that will result in any major negative consequences.

But when fear begins to interfere with our life and results in avoiding doing things we really want to do, then we need to pay attention. ... Some fear is good. It helps us recognize danger so that we can protect ourselves.

Psychologists define resilience as the process of adapting well in the face of adversity, trauma, tragedy, threats, or significant sources of stress—such as family and relationship problems, serious health problems, or workplace and financial stressors. ... That's the role of resilience.

How Facing Fear Builds Resilience

If the fear or anxiety is milder, you can try mindfulness meditation techniques. All you need to do is sit quietly and observe the present moment. If fear or anxiety arises, recognize it. Note that anytime you feel too agitated to be curious, it may be best to stop and open your eyes and notice objects in the room or take a little walk.

Life has a way of throwing countless opportunities at us to strengthen our resilience.

Why do some people seem to be better able to cope in these troubling times than others? While everyone's situation is different, it is true that people with resilience tend to have a higher tolerance for the emotional distress generated by hard times. The more resilient you are, the better you're able to tolerate the feelings of stress, anxiety, and sadness that accompany trauma and adversity—and find a way to rebound from setbacks.

We all go through bad times, experience disappointment, loss, and change, and we all feel sad, anxious, and stressed at various times in our lives. But building resilience can help you maintain a positive outlook, face an uncertain future with less fear, and get through even the darkest days.

If you're more sensitive to emotional distress and are finding it difficult to cope with hardship or adversity, it's important not to think of it as some kind of character flaw. Resilience isn't a macho quality, and it isn't fixed; it's an ongoing process that requires effort to build and maintain over time.

Unless you've faced adversity in your life before, it's unlikely you've had the need or opportunity to develop resilience. Drawing on past experiences can help you cope with the challenges you're facing today.

While it's often difficult to imagine anything good coming out of traumatic experiences, building resilience can help you find any positives in the difficulties you've faced. Surviving hardships can teach you important things about yourself and the world around you, strengthen your resolve, deepen your empathy, and in time enable you to evolve and grow as a human being.

Develop Mindset

Resilience is the ability to adapt and bounce back when things don't go as planned. Being resilient in some situations can even build inner strength and boost confidence in many areas of life. Being able to thrive despite experiencing challenging events or situations can appear to be easier for some of us than others. Being resilient is to experience challenges or adversity and absorb these into your own experience.

Whether in sports, business, academics, or entertainment, having a success mindset is important to succeed in today's world. Individuals with a success mindset always seem to figure out things to happen with their resilience, grit, and determination despite the adverse situation. There are ample examples of people with a success mindset with difficult upbringings who have made notable achievements in life. There are leaders who have managed to fight unbelievable circumstances and secure success. The only difference is the difference of mindset, also called success mindset.

Another aspect of a successful mindset is to believe in the positive possibilities for yourself, which does not mean to believe that you can do everything. But if you can realize the positive possibility that you can improve step-by-step and become a better version of yourself, this is the belief that positive changes can happen when you take steps to make it happen.

Having the right mindset is the key to success. Although hard work, effort, and persistence are all important, but not as important as having that underlying belief that you are in control of your own destiny.

Mindset will always prompt you for another fight to win, meaning no matter what the size or big your problems are, don't give up; instead, face it.

How Does Mindset Improve Resilience?

Building resilience is all about maintaining a positive mindset, a willingness to grow, and an ability to learn from setbacks. Setting goals and making time for reflection have been shown to help maintain focus and create momentum in times of growth and change. Breaking down situations, issues, or assessments into smaller, less intimidating chunks can make it easier for students to stay in a positive mindset. They are less likely to be deterred by setbacks. Creating environments where students feel confident to discuss what they want to achieve and their strategies for doing it is important in helping them to build resilience.

Mindset Plays Crucial Role in Building Resilience. A growth mindset can help protect you against psychological problems, such as depression, behavior problems, school disengagement, burnout, and other negative outcome variables. Resilience might be the critical factor in reaching the objective of positive education.

A resilient mindset helps to build self-confidence and self-esteem. When you work through difficult circumstances and overcome successfully, you improve your resilience. Just as a muscle gets stronger when lifting a weight, your resilience grows with each obstacle you overcome.

Building better resilience takes time, effort, commitment, and focus. It's a process that will take months to learn and master. Don't give up and lose your patience. Resilience is a skill that you can readily enhance with patience and training.

Many leaders feel unbelievably stretched and stressed beyond their limits, like tired rubber bands that no longer return to their original position. So how do you increase your elasticity so you can naturally return to a balanced state? Resiliency is the elastic force we use to return to normal when stress and crisis stretch us out. Unlike rubber bands, as humans, we have the ability to build resiliency. We build our resiliency in times of crisis and stress by seeing these moments as opportunities to develop this critical leadership skill. Leaders can become more effective, calmer under pressure, and rebound faster from destabilizing challenges by developing a resilient mindset.

The belief that you can always grow is called the growth mindset. If you have a growth mindset, you know that you need to practice to become good at something. If you get negative feedback, you know that you can use that feedback to grow, and that feedback doesn't say something about you that you can't change. When you make a mistake with a growth mindset, you can understand that mistakes can actually help you grow.

Having the right mindset means that you are more likely to adapt and try hard to keep growing and learning. We learned that our brain is like a muscle that grows stronger with exercise. Nobody expects anyone to be able to run a marathon or lift a heavy weight without practicing, but just like you can grow those muscles, you can also grow your brain. This can help people achieve better results, and pursue their goals, and dream big dreams for their lives.

Physical Fitness And Resilience

Do you really believe that physical fitness has any role in developing a person's resilience? It does. Resilience is the ability to withstand, recover, and grow during stress and changing demands. Resilience is the result of a complex series of internal and external characteristics, including genetics, physical fitness, mental health, and environment. Among all the factors for the development of resilience, physical activity/exercise has been considered to play an important role. Physical fitness is one pathway toward resilience because it is associated with many traits and attributes required for resilience. Physical fitness, achieved through regular exercise or physical activities, confers resilience because regular exercise or physical activity induces positive psychological benefits, protects against the potential consequences of stressful events, and prevents many chronic diseases. Physical exercise induces many positive effects on the brain and represents an important tool to influence neurodevelopment and shape the adult brain to react to life's challenges.

Resilience is known as bouncing back from adversities and bringing in strength to cope with difficulties. Adversities happen on the personal front many times in life. Resilience allows the person to come out of the adversity and move forward further. This is a way of maintaining positive mental health and maintaining one's own well-being amidst adverse conditions. It enables a person to maintain positive health in the midst of challenges.

Nowadays, it is advised to engage in physical activities to improve our health and reduce the risk of chronic disease. Engaging in physical activity helps your body recover psychologically and physically. In addition, when you do physical activities, it improves your mood, reduces anxiety and depression, and makes your brain more resilient to stress. In short, physical activity and fitness play a protective role in developing stress-related disorders.

To be resilient, we need to stay calm. If you are physically weak and suffering physical pain, would you stay calm or listen to advise? Only a strong person can stay calm, which is the precondition to think and act appropriately. The only way for you to become a strong person is to learn how to become strong before something bad happens; physical fitness is one of them. A physically fit person is able to withstand hardships and recover quickly from difficult conditions.

Everybody has a dream, but not everyone has a plan, and fewer still have the intelligence and strength to execute the plan successfully. A perfect plan is useless if you don't have the intelligence and strength to execute it. You can learn how to be resilient.

How To Improve Physical Fitness?

Your body is a big part of influencing your thoughts and impacting your success. With the increase in age, your alertness slowly gets reduced. Working out helps decrease that speed and keeps you alert. You should participate in activities and hobbies you enjoy, including physical activity in your daily routine, plenty of sleep, eating a healthy diet, and practicing stress management and relaxation techniques, such as yoga, meditation, breathing or prayer, etc.

Sleep is essential to become fit physically and mentally. Make a habit of proper sleep and develop better sleeping patterns. Having enough rest and getting adequate hours of sleep is highly recommended, especially with teenagers. Individuals need 7-8 hours of sleep every night to function optimally. If you have enough hours of sleep, you can be sure that you are one step closer to becoming emotionally and mentally healthy.

Try and be more physically active, and exercise regularly. When you take care of your body, you are better able to cope effectively with challenges in your life. It is a fact that regular exercise can help you quickly get rid of stress and at the same time it can lift up your mood. According to studies, exercise is considered to be a powerful antidote for depression, anxiety, and stress. Most of us are aware of the many physical benefits of exercise, such as strength and fitness, maintaining a healthy weight, and protecting us from chronic diseases like heart disease, cancer, and diabetes. But did you know that regular exercise has positive effects on brain function and mental health – reducing risk for dementia, anxiety, and depression while improving mood, improving sleep, and building resilience to stress. You can look for simple ways to add exercise into your daily activities, such as taking the stairs of your house instead of using the elevator or going on short walks. If you want to experience the fantastic benefits of being emotionally and mentally healthy, 30 minutes of daily exercise can be great.

Stress is just as physical as it is emotional. Promoting positive lifestyle factors like proper nutrition, ample sleep, hydration, and regular exercise can strengthen your body to adapt to stress and reduce the toll of emotions like anxiety or depression. Remaining focused in the face of stress and adversity is essential but not easy. Stress-reduction techniques, such as guided imagery, breathing exercise, and mindfulness training, can help individuals regulate their emotions, thoughts, and behaviors.

You need to learn how to have a well-balanced diet. A lot of people are unaware of how large of role nutrition actually plays in our moods and our mental health. It may be difficult for you to follow this diet initially, but it will surely pay off in the long run. Make sure to eat a more balanced and healthy diet.

Research studies have shown that people who exercise regularly are more likely to have a better cognitive function (memory, focus, thinking skills) than those who don't exercise. This has been found for middle and old-age people, where regular physical exercise is associated with better cognitive function and less age-related brain shrinkage.

Acquiring greater resilience is like a muscle that can be exercised and made even stronger.

Maintain An Optimistic Outlook

Hope is the expectation of a better tomorrow. The hopeful people are happier, healthier, and even live longer. It is common for most people to feel optimistic on good days, but it is equally important to stay positive on rainy days. Staying optimistic during dark periods can be difficult, but maintaining a hopeful outlook is integral to resiliency. What you are dealing with may be painful, but it's important to remain hopeful and positive about a brighter future.

Optimism is a tendency to expect good things in the future. Optimism is a mental attitude that heavily influences physical and mental health and coping with everyday social and working life. Through adaptive management of personal goals and development and active coping tactics, optimists are significantly more successful than pessimists in aversive events and when important life goals are impaired.

It's always hard to be positive when life is not going your way. A hopeful outlook empowers you to expect that good thing will happen to you. This is optimism. You should try visualizing what you want rather than worrying about what you fear. Along the way, note any subtle ways you start to feel better as you deal with testing situations.

Positive thinking does not mean ignoring the problem to focus on positive outcomes. It means understanding that setbacks are temporary and that you have the skills and abilities to combat the challenges you face.

What Is Optimism?

Optimism is like an engine that powers resiliency. We may possess many strengths, but that will not work unless supported by deep-rooted optimism. Sometimes, we get impacted worst in health or relationship, or work. Still, this powerful trait supports the unyielding belief that even our darkest hours bring with them hope and empowerment to get over the severe challenges.

As per Renee Branson, Author, "Optimism is the fuel and the faith that drives our resilience when our other resilience tools (reason, composure, vision) are temporarily out of reach. Optimism is the chair we sink into that we know will hold us until reason and composure catch up."

People can have different levels of optimism over time, and one's degree of optimism can change depending on the context or situation. Healthy optimism allows people to identify and take advantage of opportunities that lead to growth and success. It may also help people maintain better mental health through stressful or difficult times.

Optimistic thinking is correlated with better mental health. For instance, people experiencing depression tend to be overwhelmed by negative, pessimistic thoughts that increase the level of depression. Researchers have investigated how optimism affects physical health as well as mental well-being. Optimism benefits physical health by establishing positive expectations. For instance, a person who believes they have the power to improve their health may be more likely to successfully improve their health than someone who does not believe in their ability to improve their health.

Why Is Optimism Essential?

When you have optimism, the rate of chances of success increases four to five times compared to when you are not optimistic because optimists keep on trying. Optimism is a better choice. Optimism helps develop your psychological strength and resilience, which sails you through when times get tough.

Professor Jane Burns - "People talk about tenacity and resilience and strength of character, but it is optimism that drives behavior when on some days it would be easier to say "stop - I give up, it's too hard. Optimism is believing in the impossible and then taking steps to make it possible."

It's the belief that no matter what challenges a person faces, he can make a difference with optimism. Optimism underpins resilience, grit, and determination.

Once a person views the world through a distressed lens, he recognizes the importance of facing harsh realities and resilience to move through and overcome the situation. Optimism helps a person not just survive but thrive through uncertain times.

Optimism significantly influences mental and physical well-being by adaptive behaviors, greater flexibility, problem-solving capacity, and an efficient understanding of negative information.

Optimistic people tend to have more positive thoughts, be more hopeful, and view the future in a positive light. When a situation is neutral, an optimistic person will be more likely to see it as positive, while a pessimistic person is more likely to see it as negative. Optimistic people also tend to see positive aspects of frustrating situations. Optimistic thinking can be a one-time event; it can also be a strategy for coping with stress or a personality trait.

Learning to be optimistic is more complex than just "focusing on the positive." Developing a more optimistic perspective typically involves recognizing personal difficulties and then thinking about them in ways that support growth and resilience. Additionally, parents can help children learn optimism by modeling behaviors that reflect a positive frame of mind.

How To Practice Optimism?

Optimism increases the chances of making good things happen now and in the future. While you might tend to have either an optimistic or pessimistic explanatory style, there are things that you can do the help cultivate a more optimistic attitude.

Becoming more mindful can be a helpful technique to help you focus on what matters in the present and avoid worrying about future events and things outside of your control. If you are living fully in the moment, you are much less likely to get influenced by negative past experiences or fear about future events. This allows you to feel more appreciative of what you have now with fewer regrets and anxieties.

If you practice gratitude, it increases optimism and resilience. If you are trying to develop a more optimistic attitude, set aside a few minutes each day to jot down some of the things you are grateful for.

Regularly writing down positive thoughts helps improve your optimism. One study found that expressive writing focused on positive emotions was linked to decreased mental distress and improved mental well-being.

Optimism is the tendency to anticipate favorable outcomes. The expression "The glass is half full" often refers to optimistic thinking.

Finally, a positive attitude helps you cope with the daily affairs of life more easily. It brings optimism into life and helps to avoid worries and negative thinking. If you bring positivity to your life and make constructive changes, you will be happier, brighter, and more successful. It is undoubtedly a state of mind that is well worth developing.

Develop Problem Solving Skills To Improve Resilience

People face problems in their everyday lives, which can occur even in the natural environment. It can be a social problem, relationship problem, and problem at work or even regarding your financial status. Sometimes people make wrong decisions for solving problems in haste. You need problem-solving skills to resolve issues that hinder your work.

Resilience is an individual's capacity to cope with, adapt to, and recover from situations of adversity. This ability varies from person to person, is influenced by biological, social, and environmental factors, and can be taught and imbibed through the proper training and skill development.

Resilience is our ability to recover quickly from hardships that we experience. Strong problem-solving skills help to look at problems comprehensively, break them down into pieces, and find solutions for them timely. A person with strong problem-solving skills becomes a more resilient person. This is because the better you are at evaluating and solving the problems in your lives, the quicker you can recover from the issues you face.

Resilience And Problem-Solving Skills

Resilient People have effective and efficient problem-solving skills, and they are able to understand a situation better, identify the issue correctly, and create a better solution. People who are able to come up with solutions to a problem are better able to cope with problems than those who cannot. Whenever a person with strong problem-solving skills encounters a new challenge, he prepares a list of some potential ways to solve the problem. If you practice problem-solving skills regularly, you will be better prepared to cope when a serious challenge emerges.

Albert Einstein said, "It's not that I'm so smart, it's just that I stay with problems longer." Einstein was perhaps highly resilient and had the ability to look at problems comprehensively. It is believed that how you think about challenges and problems can help you build resilience at work. This is because the better you are at evaluating and solving the problems that arise in your lives, the quicker you can recover from the issues you face.

One can develop resilience by developing themselves more independently. This can only occur through taking responsibility, becoming accountable, and being free of dependence. Activities, when done independently, develop self-confidence and a sense of confidence in dealing with problems. When a person solves problems, he/she acquire the skills to face life and adversity.

How To Develop Strong Problem-Solving Skills

In order to become more resilient, you must learn to strengthen problem-solving skills so you can deal with obstacles in a better way. The following are ways to develop problem-solving skills:-

Ask Questions

Asking questions is one of the best ways to develop strong problem-solving skills because asking questions gets you to begin thinking critically. One stimulates critical thinking to get to the bottom of problems and begins developing solutions by asking analytical questions. Asking questions also ensures that the problem is accurately defined to address the correct issue.

Gather Information

Information is the strength and gives us a clue to solving the problem. The information helps us make a strong foundation for the problem to be accurately defined and solved.

Flexibility & Adaptability

The ability to be flexible is an important skill to possess when it comes to problem-solving. This means, to get possible solutions, one may realize that selected options are not viable and need to go with other options to more effectively solve the problem.

Approach Problem with Positivity

Often, people approach problems with apprehension and negativity. That hinders their ability to address an issue. When you have a positive outlook, you can approach issues with optimism. That makes us more likely actually to find a viable solution. Approaching the problem on a positive note also helps find the solution easily. Being worried about whether the problem can be solved sometimes makes grave mistakes while finding solutions. Keeping calm will help you to think and evaluate the problem more effectively.

Believing that a challenge is an opportunity for growth and a positive outcome can be achieved sets the tone for the ultimate outcome.

So, when you are better equipped to solve problems, you become more resilient. Having the skills to analyze issues, generate possible options, and apply solutions also helps you build more tolerance of difficulties and recover from the difficulties you face with speed.

Thus, active pursuit of activities and opportunities that will allow you to practice asking more questions, gathering information, being flexible, and approaching problems with positivity will help build better problem-solving skills and therefore enhance your resilience.

At work and in life, problems can crop up. Even if you don't know how to fix the problem at first, you should keep calm, think about how the problem happened, and logically try to find some good solutions.

This rational way of looking at things with a clear head is called problem-solving. Life will always have problems to overcome, from figuring out why your phone isn't working to dealing with challenges at home and the workplace.

Self-Discovery

In the journey of life, everyone has to grow with time in terms of values, knowledge, skills, attitude, mental strength, gratitude, etc. Everyone faces challenges, and without resilience, it is very challenging to progress in life. Developing your resilience is all about small and simple steps and requires practice. Self-discovery is one of them. Self-discovery is nothing but understanding more about yourself, your weakness, and strengths, and keep learning and upgrading yourself on a regular basis.

Self-discovery is about learning something new. It could be a skill or an interest that you continue developing and striving for your goals. People often lack time for non-development, which is just a lame excuse and is a self-defeating attitude.

In fact, it is always better to acknowledge and accept emotions during hard times to foster self-discovery by asking yourself, "What can I do about a problem in my life?" If the problems seem too big, the best way to tackle them is to break them down into manageable pieces.

For instance, if you have a hard time at work, you may not convince your superior to forgive your mistake and let you go. But you can spend an hour each day developing your top strengths or working on your skills to make you stronger. Taking the initiative motivates during stressful periods of your life, increasing the likelihood of getting over your painful times.

People learn quickly as a result of their challenges in life. The bigger the challenges, the bigger the learning. Many people who have experienced tragedies and hardship have reported better perseverance, better relationships, a greater sense of accountability, an increased sense of self-worth, a more developed spirituality, and an intensified gratitude for life.

When you go deep with yourself and with someone who has the same level of frequency, you can self-discover yourself with a strong purpose and meaningful life.

Have you ever thought deeply about exactly what you want from life? Dreams, personal values, talents, even your personality traits may not get preferences much in busy daily life. But awareness of these characteristics can give you plenty of insight into your inner self.

Self-discovery is a lifelong journey of exploration through our inner self, trying to discover who we are, our potential, our purpose in life, and what core principles are guiding us to take different paths along the way. The journey starts with self-awareness, then explores personal interests, hopes, and dreams for the future. The journey eventually leads us to self-knowledge, enabling us to guide ourselves towards situations and experiences in which we will thrive.

Self-discovery is a fundamental component of personal growth. We must take the time to discover who we are as a person. Self-discovery is a way to explore our individual personalities, national preferences, feelings, values, beliefs, emotions, and tendencies. Since we see all different in the way we think, feel, act, learn, and perceive the world, it is beneficial to take the time to reflect in order to gain a better insight into ourselves. Self-discovery is a way for us to explore our individual personalities, natural preferences, values, beliefs, preferred styles, and tendencies. The ultimate destination of this journey is finding out who we are and what makes us unique.

Day-to-day priorities are important, indeed. But a life that's nothing more than a series of going through the same motions usually doesn't provide much enjoyment.

If you've reached a point in life where you find yourself asking, "Who am I, really?" some self-discovery can help you get to know yourself a little better.

Self-discovery should be an important goal for everyone. Some people go through life playing a role to mask who they really are. Others simply become what others want them to be.

How To Do Self-Discovery?

Many people who have experienced tragedies and hardship realized in the end that those were opportunities to learn about themselves; 'what doesn't kill you, makes you stronger' is a famous quote reflecting that every failure may teach valuable lessons to ourselves.

The journey of self-discovery is both challenging and rewarding. It means exploring our strengths and weaknesses, our motivations and needs. Discovering more of our potential unlocks possibilities for being more fulfilled and engaging more in life.

There are many important questions that any individual should answer in search of happiness and freedom in his/her life. Self-discovery is actually a process that explores several areas of ourselves involving mind, body, heart, and spirit to enrich the quality of our life. What is more, discovering ourselves often requires stepping out of our comfort zone, subjecting ourselves to unfamiliar territories.

If you are not sure how to set about probing your psyche and emotional depths, the following tips can help you embark on your journey of self-discovery.

Read Self-Discovery Books

Start by getting acquainted with the concept of self-discovery. Learn the meaning of a personal inventory and how to handle what you find. Reading books about the discovery of self will open new doors of insight and understanding. Some can be read as theory or text, while others are designed as workbooks so that you can read a section and then write your thoughts.

Take Inventory

Buy a journal or notebook and set aside some time to reflect on your life so far. What have you accomplished? What are your pet peeves? Do you have any major fears? Are you struggling against certain obstacles? Have you set realistic goals? Do you enjoy occasional daydreams or fantasies? List these in categories and see which area has more. That might be the category to focus on first. Or, if you feel strong emotions about one of the areas, start with that one.

Embrace Discovery Of The Self

In assessing your personal inventory, you may feel anxious, nervous, or even a little afraid of what you could find deep within. Don't worry. Whatever lies hidden in your soul will benefit from the light of discovery. If you find negative things, like fears, doubts, or negative traits, exposure will help you deal with them once and for all. But if you find positive things, like strength, skill, or daring, don't be afraid to use them to reach your highest goals.

Simply put, accept whatever you find and continue to move forward in your quest for self-discovery. You can grow even stronger by honestly facing the characteristics revealed by your personal inventory. Don't be afraid to admit who you are and accept your limitations. Only then can you start working on the weaknesses to become a better person and enjoy your strengths to savor each day.

Experiment With Self-Discovery Activities

In addition to reading, keeping a journal, and reflecting on who you are or who you want to become, there are several additional things you can do to help you get to the root of your identity.-- Explore your spiritual side by visiting a church, synagogue, or another place of worship. Pray or meditate about the origins of the universe and your place in it. Compare your journey of the body to the journey of your soul. Reflect on your personal values and morals and why they are essential to you.--

Think about your physical being. Set a reasonable goal, such as losing two pounds per month, and stick with it. Or start walking 10 minutes daily and increase that amount of time by 10 minutes each week until you can walk for an hour. Expand your mind. Make a list of relevant books that you can read at the rate of one per month. Consider joining a book group online or in your community to discuss stimulating books. You might even change your mind on certain issues, which helps cultivate an open mind.

Benefits Of Self-Discovery

Self-discovery can help improve resilience by allowing you to gain a deeper understanding of yourself. Self-discovery can help you feel more confident and reduce or manage stress. This will also help you organize your thoughts and contemplate different aspects of your lives. Practicing self-discovery has many benefits and can effectively build resilience and strengthen your mental health. Practicing self-discovery can help you do the following:

- Assists to understand your strengths and boosting self-confidence
- It helps to clarify your goals and purpose and action plan to work towards them
- Supports to identify your weaknesses so that you can improve
- Assess your present situation and your reaction to different situations and people
- Assists to develop greater emotional intelligence
- Helps to make decisions, create solutions for the challenges and create an action plan
- Make you stronger, focused, and resilient

How to Practice Self-Discovery

Self-discovery helps develop self-awareness, which can help you to work towards self-acceptance. You will get a clear picture of who you are and where you are at can really help you understand where you are heading for. If you want to change your path, self-discovery can help you visualize and understand how to do so. Self-discovery will help you find clarity and start creating the life you desire.

You need to allocate some time aside during the week or month to practice self-discovery. You can also practice this in your routine or use this technique when you are feeling overwhelmed.

Practicing Self-discovery involves certain specific questions. Depending on the situation you want to address, there are specific questions you can ask yourself. It is important to answer questions honestly and without judging yourself. Answers should be spontaneous without defending yourself. Always remember that you are doing this to reflect and grow. Therefore, answer how you really feel, not how you think you should feel.

Conclusion

We have learned so much about resilience and how it impacts our success. This book has given a bird's eye view of building resilience to face the challenges in life and become successful. There will be times in all of your lives when pressures mount, or you experience pain and trauma at a point; it isn't easy to manage. However, through learning about yourselves and realizing what you can and cannot manage, you will be able to develop strategies that allow you to become resilient, take these difficulties in your stride, and feel confident in your abilities to manage. It will be effective if you read thoroughly, understand and implement all actionable points. Remember that building resilience is a learnable skill and one of the critical factors in success.

May I Ask A Small Favor?

At the outset, I would like to thank you for taking out time to read this book. You could have chosen any other book, but you took mine, and I appreciate this.

I hope you got at least a few actionable insights that will positively impact your life.

I'd love it if you could leave a review for the book. Reviews may not matter to big-name authors, but these are a tremendous help for amateur authors like me, who don't have much following.

I sincerely request you to leave your review at the platform directly.

Thanks for supporting my work.

Disclaimer

Although the publisher and the author have made every effort to ensure that the information in this book is correct, and while this publication is designed to provide accurate information regarding the subject matter covered, the publisher and the author assume no responsibility for errors, inaccuracies, omissions, or any other inconsistencies herein and hereby disclaim any liability to any party for any loss, damage, or disruption caused by errors or omissions, and whether such errors or omissions result from negligence, accident, or any other cause.

The ideas, procedures, and suggestions in this book are not intended as a substitute for consulting with an expert. Neither the author nor the publisher shall be liable or responsible for any loss or damage allegedly arising from any information or suggestion in this book.

Copyright @ 2021 Pradip N Das

Gratitude

This book is dedicated to all my well-wishers whose continuous support helped me write another book on success.

I sincerely thank all my readers who inspired me with their love and appreciation for my previous books.

Jn

9 789358 108316